CONTENTS

FOREWORD

THIS is the eighth in a series of occasional papers published by Learning Unlimited, and now collected under the general title, *The Learning Teacher*. It continues the original purpose of bringing teachers up-to-date with what we now know about how children learn and how effective teachers teach.

A doctor who had failed to keep up-to-date with medical developments over the past twenty years would have a quiet surgery. Yet in education, many teachers have now been in post for longer than that without receiving similar opportunities to update their knowledge about learning and teaching.

These papers summarise our best understandings to date about how we learn and how best to help other people learn. We still have a lot to discover but our knowledge is growing rapidly thanks to advances in neurology, psychology and, not least, good classroom practice.

At the end of a busy day, most teachers have neither time nor energy to read lengthy academic texts. So the papers in *The Learning Teacher* series are short, readable and comprehensive: they 'do the reading for you' and those with particularly enquiring minds are directed to further reading at the end.

This paper is devoted to assessment and draws heavily on the work of Paul Black and Dylan Wiliam at King's College in London.

Their pamphlet, *Inside the Black Box: Raising standards through classroom assessment* is one of the best reviews of research literature I have ever seen. It refers to 580 articles published over nine years in more than 160 academic journals. Black and Wiliam included only robust research with findings verified, for example, by the use of control groups.

When we look back in ten years' time, I believe *Inside the Black Box* will be seen as one of the most influential books on education for a generation. Since assessment is a key factor in improving the quality of learning and teaching in our schools today, so its insights and wisdom are of lasting value to us all.

I am grateful to all my colleagues at Learning Unlimited for their support in writing this paper and to those in the field who took the time to read drafts and comment on them, particularly George Sinclair and Alan McLean. Finally my thanks to Eric Young for the excellent job he did in editing and producing the paper.

Ian Smith, September 2003

I   ASSESSMENT IS A DIRTY WORD

Assessment can be enormously constructive in teaching and learning and also enormously destructive.
Pollard and Tann

ASSESSMENT is essential to effective teaching. Good teachers constantly assess learning, sometimes explicitly, sometimes in the bustle of a busy classroom. They recognise the need to try to tune into learners' minds, to work out what and how they are thinking and to use this to stimulate progress.

Yet in education, assessment has always been fraught with difficulty. Derek Rowntree who wrote one of the best books on the subject as long ago as 1977, said:

> *"The assessment debate is awash with hidden assumptions, unstated views, partial truths, confusions of ideas, false distinctions, and irrelevant emphases. It is also flooded with jargon".*

Since then, things seem only to have got worse. Recently Torrance and Pryor quoted an LEA adviser who described assessment as *"a dirty word for teachers"*. Having run courses for teachers on many aspects of learning and teaching over the past ten years, I know that sessions on assessment have not been popular.

Hopefully, times are changing. Through the work of Dylan Wiliam and Paul Black at Kings College in London, the Assessment Reform Group in England and Wales and the Scottish 'Assessment is for Learning' programme, formative assessment – assessment for learning – is back on the map. Teachers are beginning to recognise an enormously constructive side of assessment, which can help them to be better teachers and their pupils better learners.

This paper is about how and why formative assessment works. It will look at what we mean by assessment for learning, why it is important and the key principles and ideas underpinning it. We will also spend some time on its current status and then go on to consider four practical strategies for using it with learners.

But first we must reflect on why the assessment scene got so bad in the first place. A renaissance for genuinely constructive assessment will only be successful if it can sit alongside and be reconciled with assessment for other purposes at national, school and classroom level.

2

HIGH-JACKED BY THE STANDARDS AGENDA

TO understand why assessment has become a dirty word for many teachers we need to think briefly on events in education over the past 25 years and their impact on assessment.

We assess for three main purposes (see panel 1). All are important and none is going to disappear. But in the past 25 years, the second two purposes have been emphasised to the detriment of the first. Indeed some would say assessment for learning has been stifled by assessment for accountability.

Concerns about educational standards, particularly in literacy and numeracy, have been the cause. The controversy in education provoked by the standards debate can be traced back to Jim Callaghan's Ruskin College speech thirty years ago. Since then, raising standards has become a centrepiece of national education policy across the political divide.

A polarised and simplistic debate over falling standards has focused on who is responsible and what can be done about it. As a consequence, there have been attempts to make schools and teachers more accountable, through, for example, league tables comparing examination results.

In England and Wales, funding for schools is more bound up with achieving good examination results than ever before. The push to raise standards has also led to a proliferation of testing and examinations. In April 2003, The Observer reported the findings of a parliamentary committee, that, *"school pupils are so overloaded by the number of exams they have to take each year that the system is in danger of a total breakdown"*.

At present, English and Welsh children face 87 tests during their school career, the first within seven weeks of starting at the age of four or five. The pressure to perform in these tests is so great that even promising pupils can find stress overwhelming them.

The burden of testing and the perceived need to keep written records of achievement for summative assessment has had a detrimental effect on teachers, too. It has taken time away from quality interaction between teacher and pupil and has undermined the role and importance of assessment for learning.

National documents helping teachers to use assessment for learning more systematically have largely been ignored or sidelined (notably *Assessment 5-14, SOED 1992* in Scotland, and *TGAT 1988* in England and Wales).

Many teachers claim that the push to raise standards through external testing has narrowed the curriculum and constrained teaching. One respondent in the columns of the Times Educational Supplement put it simply: *"What happened to imagination? What happened to integrity? What happened to fun? What happened?"*

So assessment is not just a technical issue; it has become political and extremely emotive, associated with very powerful feelings of helplessness, insecurity, guilt, frustration and anger. Teachers believe recent initiatives have made a difficult job harder. Worse still, they believe they have been introduced because the profession is no longer trusted.

Panel 1

Why do we assess and who is it for?

■ **To support learning**
(mainly for pupils and their class teachers)

- sometimes called formative assessment,
- usually diagnostic and on-going,
- usually focuses on soft as well as hard indicators and takes account of teachers' intuitive judgements and knowledge of the whole child,
- prime purpose of giving pupils feedback to help them see how they are doing and how they might improve,
- also useful to teachers to help them know how best to support pupils and adapt their teaching approaches,
- research indicates improvements in motivation and self-esteem.

■ **For review, transfer and certification**
(mainly for parents, employers and other teachers)

- summative assessment,
- tends to be a review or overview of previous learning,
- tends to use hard indicators, neglecting soft indicators and a picture of the whole child,
- can help pupils learn but can also have negative effects on learning,
- satisfies parents' wishes to be aware of how their children are doing at school,
- facilitates transition from pre-school to primary, primary to secondary and secondary to college or university,
- helps teachers to provide opportunities for progression from year to year and stage to stage.

■ **For informing school improvement and public accountability**
(mainly for parents, managers and politicians)

- summative assessment,
- tends to be a collecting together of evidence of the performance of a group of learners,
- usually focuses almost exclusively on hard rather than soft indicators,
- used by parents to select a school for their child,
- used by managers and administrators and inspectors to judge a school or an individual teacher's performance,
- does not take account of the research which indicates that school is responsible for about 15% of the achievement of pupils.

The headlines below illustrate the emotional impact of assessment on parents and young people, too. Yet we should remember that public accountability is important. We should be interested in standards because schools and teachers have to answer to society for what they do. However, when good intentions produce unplanned negative results they must be addressed before they threaten the very standards they are supposed to improve. No-one has demonstrated this more effectively than Paul Black and Dylan Wiliam and it is to their work we will turn in the next two sections.

FIVE YEAR OLDS TAGGED AS FAILURES
September 1998

I am useless and I am three
SATS ARE MEANINGLESS AND DESTROY PUPILS'
CONFIDENCE. THEY MUST GO.
June 2002

THIS EXAM MADNESS
WHILE THE GOVERNMENT INSISTS ON PUTTING TESTING
BEFORE LEARNING, CHILDREN WILL ALWAYS BE THE LOSERS.
June 2002

SCHOOLS CHEAT TO BOOST EXAM RESULTS
CHILDREN AND TEACHERS TESTIFY TO THE CHEATING
June 2002

EXAM SYSTEM FACES OVERLOAD CRISIS
April 2003

3   HARMFUL SIDE EFFECTS

There is a wealth of research evidence that the everyday practice of assessment in classrooms is beset with problems and shortcomings.
Paul Black and Dylan Wiliam *Inside the Black Box*

MILITARY strategists warn us that all wars produce unintended results, usually harmful and damaging to the expected outcome. The same is true of educational initiatives. Black and Wiliam's message is that there is a real danger that the national efforts to raise standards in schools will actually have the opposite effect.

Their research is not alone in showing that undermining assessment for learning threatens the very educational standards we all want. A focus on summative assessment can be harmful in different ways that have been widely reported in the UK and abroad:

Harmful to learning

Classroom assessment has become disconnected from learning. For many teachers, it is mainly about measurement through paper and pencil tests, administered by the teacher after learning has taken place with the aim of assigning a pupil to an appropriate level or grade:

> *"It's very much a tick on sheet, we've covered the work and then move onto the next thing. It's not really tied into how the child is doing in themselves, with their interests and how they could go forward or with what their particular needs are."*
> **Primary 1 teacher in England quoted in Torrance and Pryor (1998)**

This describes a tendency to emphasise the end product, the quality of the presentation or the marks gained out of ten and to neglect the process and what it can tell us about how children are learning.

Also the plethora of tests has affected what and how we teach. There has been a huge emphasis on teaching literacy and numeracy out of context and at the expense of other areas. This, in turn, promotes an emphasis on covering content and accumulating knowledge through rote and superficial learning at the expense of encouraging thinking and developing understanding.

Harmful to teaching

Black and Wiliam's findings suggest that classroom assessment has become a management tool for teachers and schools, serving social and managerial functions often at the expense of learning functions. It is about how children are assigned to classes or to groups within classes, for example, rather than helping them to improve and succeed as individuals.

There is also a great pressure on teachers to assess collectively and according to a schedule rather than use the process of assessment to help individual children learn. Yet we all recognise that children do not learn and develop uniformly to any national timetable.

Another pressure on teachers is to teach to the test. In Scotland, where teachers can decide when to administer the test, teachers are keen to avoid their classes being tested until they can perform in a way that will reflect well on their own judgement. Throughout the UK, teachers can often predict pupils' results on external tests because their own classroom tests imitate them, but at the same time they know too little about pupils' learning needs, because collecting marks to fill up records is given priority over analysing pupils' work to discern learning needs.

Finally there is great debate about the reliability of tests and both teachers and schools are tempted to administer their own rather than rely on the tests administered by a previous teacher, perhaps at a different school. To show the value it has added, a school will argue that it needs an accurate baseline to start from.

Harmful to learners

The most significant and worrying finding of the King's College research however is that an overemphasis on summative assessment has a negative impact on learners and especially underachievers lacking confidence in their own ability.

They point out that where giving marks and grades is overemphasised and useful advice under-emphasised, assessment can all too readily be about communicating failure rather than supporting progress. Also where pupils are compared with one another too often, the prime motivation becomes competition, not personal improvement. When feedback tells pupils with low attainment that they lack 'ability', they become demotivated.

In the years since *Inside the Black Box* was published, these findings have been reiterated in other ways. More and more, we are appreciating the importance of motivation in learning. In his book, *Wise Up*, Guy Claxton says self-confidence or resilience contributes more to successful learning than ability. A belief in their own ability and the roles of teachers and schools in fostering these beliefs are also important factors for children.

Alan McLean, in *The Motivated School*, discusses the impact of what he calls achievement mindsets. He identifies four that we all share. Two of them, the 'mastery mindset' and the 'performance mindset' are positive and help us to try to succeed. Two of them, the 'self-worth protection' mindset and the 'learned helplessness' mindset, are negative and encourage us simply to avoid failure. McLean's work demonstrates why an assessment system that measures and compares can lead many children, even those with a performance mindset, to seek only to avoid failure and to 'retire hurt' from school (panel 2).

Panel 2

Retiring hurt – Assessment and Motivation

Where the classroom focuses on rewards, 'gold stars', grades or place-in-the-class ranking, then pupils look for the ways to obtain the best marks, rather than at the needs of their learning which these marks ought to reflect. Or they seek to 'get by' and avoid difficult tasks. Or, even worse, they simply give up and 'retire hurt'.
Black and Wiliam *Inside the Black Box*

To prevent pupils from 'retiring hurt', we need to create a culture of success, backed by a belief that all can achieve. One way to do this is to ensure that feedback to any pupil is about the particular qualities of his or her work, with advice on what he or she can do to improve, and avoids comparison with others.
Black and Wiliam *Inside the Black Box*

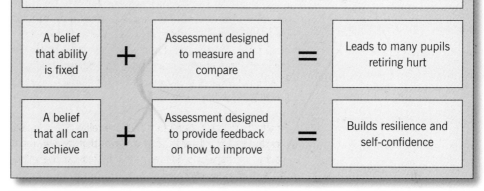

4   A NEW EMPHASIS: THE KEY IDEAS

Recent research shows that innovations, which include the strengthening of formative assessment, produce significant and often substantial learning gains, over ages, subjects and countries. Many studies show that it benefits low attainers in particular.
Paul Black and Dylan Wiliam *Inside the Black Box*

Assessment for learning raises standards of achievement

BLACK AND WILIAM called for a new emphasis on assessment for learning. They did so because their research showed that formative assessment can have a positive effect on learning and teaching and so raise standards of performance in classrooms and schools. The studies they reviewed range over several ages (from five year olds to university graduates), subjects and countries. They are also based on careful quantitative experiments. Learning gains are measured by comparing average improvements on test scores with the range of scores that are found for typical groups of pupils on the same tests.

The most persuasive finding for many was that several studies show that improved formative assessment helps the so-called low attainers more than the rest, reducing the spread of attainment while still raising it for everyone.

Why does it raise performance?

Why is assessment for learning so successful in getting just the results we all want?
To understand, we need to look more closely at what assessment for learning is, how it differs from summative assessment and what it actually means in classroom practice.

Black and Wiliam defined assessment for learning as follows:

> *In this paper the term 'assessment' refers to all those activities undertaken by teachers, and their students themselves, which provide information to be used as feedback to modify the teaching and learning activities in which they are engaged. Such assessment only becomes formative assessment when the evidence is actually used to adapt the teaching work to meet the needs.*
> **Paul Black and Dylan Wiliam** *Inside the Black Box*

Formative assessment, then, has a number of fundamental differences from summative assessment (see panel 3). It increases teachers' understanding of their pupils and helps them provide pupils with quality feedback to improve learning. It looks forward rather than backward: teachers can build on prior learning and pupils can act on their teacher's advice.

It is an essential part of good learning and teaching

For formative assessment to work, teachers need to focus on how children are learning. They need to tune into children's minds, to connect with their thinking and feelings. Pupils need to know what they are supposed to learn and how to identify success, so teachers need to ask themselves, 'Do I really know enough about my pupils' understandings to be able to help each one of them?'

If teachers address this challenging question then teaching and learning becomes an interactive, collaborative process, where teachers can talk with pupils, raising open-ended questions and both can then share and construct their understandings together. Teachers can also observe and listen and pupils can monitor their own work and thinking.

In other words, the rationale for formative assessment is based firmly on our growing understandings of how we learn and how good teachers teach. We know that self motivation

Panel 3

Formative assessment

Mainly about improvement

Key questions
How well are you doing?
What progress has he made?
What does she need to do now?

Tends to be forward looking: part of the learning process, on-going and continuous, used as an aid to future progress.

Mainly used to diagnose needs, to provide feedback to help learners learn and to help teachers improve teaching.

Casts teacher in the role of facilitator.

Favours the use of informal assessment instruments applied by the teacher.

These can be time-consuming to compile, complex in scoring, less easily generalised and more subjective.

Can lead to improvements in learning and teaching and provide a way of assessing a wide range of skills, qualities and attitudes.

Summative assessment

Mainly about accountability

Key questions
How good are you?
Is she at level E yet?
Can he do his six times table?

Tends to be backward looking: to come at the end of a learning process, often separate from it and indicate present or past achievement.

Mainly used to provide information to others about how much learners have learned for certification and accountability.

Casts teacher in the role of judge.

Favours the use of formal standardised tests, usually devised and sometimes scored by someone other than the teacher.

These are short, cheap, easy to score and generalise from, but usually lack validity especially when used for accountability purposes.

Where overused has a negative impact on learning and teaching and leads to a narrowing of the curriculum.

and the ability to learn how to learn are crucial (see panel 4). Formative assessment is based on constructivist models of learning and has been linked directly to Vygotsky's ideas on scaffolding, which gives teachers a key role in extending children's understanding as it develops. Classroom based formative assessment is a way of getting close to children's thinking and giving direct support to their development.

Children coached to think for themselves rather than simply being told become more resourceful and reflective, good at learning and at knowing what works for them and what doesn't. Resourceful, reflective children perform more effectively in examinations. It's hardly surprising therefore that assessment for learning raises achievement.

It motivates through success

For underachievers who lack self-belief and self-esteem, assessment for learning can motivate because it helps children to realise that it's okay to be wrong or only partially understand something and that they can be successful through their own efforts. Assessment for learning helps a teacher to work with learners, without the risk of doing the learning to them or for them.

But helping teachers to work this way presents a real challenge. We must now turn to practical strategies.

Panel 4

Assessment for learning – Key ideas

Assessment can help all children be more motivated if teachers:

- emphasise real progress and achievement rather than failure,
- praise effort rather than ability,
- emphasise progress against previous personal best and avoid or play down comparisons with others,
- are aware of the effect comments, marks and grades can have on learners' confidence and self-esteem.

Assessment can help all children to learn if teachers:

- are clear with learners about what they are being asked to learn and how they will know they have been successful,
- help them become more aware of how as well as what they're learning,
- help them to reflect on their strengths and weaknesses,
- give them guidance on how to improve and opportunities to do so.

5 MAKING IT WORK IN PRACTICE: THE KEY STRATEGIES

Teachers do not need to choose between being a good teacher and getting good results.
Dylan Wiliam

MAKING assessment for learning work in a school or classroom is a challenge. A large body of evidence may say that it leads to higher quality learning, but the pressure on schools to improve the results achieved by pupils in national tests and examinations often precludes its use. Many teachers feel that, to get such results, you have to teach from the front and teach to the test.

As a follow-up to *Inside the Black Box*, Dylan Wiliam and others at King's College demonstrated that teachers could improve the quality of assessment for learning in their classrooms within the existing constraints of national tests and examinations. Their results were reported to the annual conference of BERA in September 2001. Some of the strategies used were also published in 2002 in *'Working Inside the Black Box'*.

The project was small: 24 teachers in six schools. Over a six-month period, they were supported to explore and plan a new approach. Then, at the start of a new session with a new class, they put into practice a new teaching programme using formative assessment. Researchers did not tell them what to do. Rather, the teachers chose from a range of options: changing their questioning techniques, developing self assessment, sharing success criteria with pupils or giving feedback and marking. In all, the 24 teachers included a total of 102 activities in their action plans. Almost every plan included reviewing questioning techniques and some form of assessment and over half mentioned using comment only marking.

The results provide evidence that formative assessment leads to tangible benefits in key stage 3 tests and GCSE. The researchers accept that the quantitative evidence generated by the project is not as sound as they would have liked, but for surprising reasons. They had intended to use as control groups other classes taught by the teacher though not using the methods being studied. However, almost all the teachers began using their new strategies with all their classes. They also claimed the project had fundamentally altered their views of themselves as professionals.

Dylan Wiliam concludes that the project showed that the choice between teaching well and getting good results is unnecessary. Since the project has ended, several of the teachers have become ambassadors for formative assessment, contributing to conferences in Scotland to support the *Assessment is for Learning* programme. This initiative replicates key aspects of the English project as part of a rationalisation of the entire system of formative and summative assessment in Scotland.

Other people have picked up the challenge of making formative assessment work in the current climate. These include Shirley Clarke, whose two eminently practical publications are included in the reading list. *The Critical Skills Programme*, promoted across the UK by Network Press, makes systematic use of formative assessment in helping children to develop team-working skills.

In Scotland, *Assessment is for Learning* was launched to take forward the strategy for developing formative assessment outlined in *Inside the Black Box* and to create an integrated approach to assessment covering other related initiatives.

The next four sections of this paper focus on the four areas where work is going on throughout the UK to explore formative assessment (panel 5).

Panel 5

Assessment for learning – Key strategies

Four practical strategies we can adopt to improve assessment for learning are:

Mark less to achieve more by...

- teaching children to do more marking themselves,
- doing less marking yourself away from children,
- making sure that the distance marking you do counts.

Tune into children's minds by...

- generating quality classroom discussions,
- establishing regular routines and rituals to encourage children to talk about how they are learning,
- involving children in stimulating activities which require them to think and talk about what they are learning.

Give immediate quality feedback that...

- is designed to be helpful and supportive
- stresses the positive but avoids plastic praise
- focuses on effort and strategies rather than products
- includes suggestions about how to improve that are important and possible

Encourage good self and peer assessment by...

- sharing learning intentions and success criteria with children,
- building self and peer assessment into classroom activities, explaining why they are doing it, making it regular and taking it seriously,
- making it lead somewhere by linking it to target and goal setting.

6   MARKING LESS TO ACHIEVE MORE

Correction usually comes too fast and too often for most learners, impressing on them precisely what they don't know and can't do.
Frank Smith

ASSESSMENT and marking are never far apart. It may seem paradoxical but one of the great practical benefits of assessment for learning worth mentioning early on is that it can release teachers from the burdens of excessive marking. Relief from the marking tyrant may well be a major incentive for teachers to explore the strategies associated with assessment for learning. If less marking can create better ways for learners to assess their own work and progress then everyone benefits.

What teachers hate about marking

Ask teachers what they hate most about marking and they will tell you; it's extremely **time consuming**, it's **boring** and **repetitive**, and, worst of all, the vast majority of marking has **little or no effect**. On the last point, many experts agree.

If teachers can follow the classic piece of advice to work smarter not harder in one area, this is it! But, in marking, the advice can be hard to take. Teachers are often stuck on the horns of a dilemma. On the one hand, they feel pressured to correct all spelling errors, to act as a copy-editor and to provide a mark and comments at the end. On the other, there is the feeling of satisfaction that comes from having been seen to do a thorough job with a red pen on a set of jotters.

Teachers, headteachers and parents need convincing of the arguments against traditional marking. Yet the evidence is strong: much marking has little positive effect and is actually responsible for regression in many pupils, since it demoralises and overwhelms them and many can make little sense of it.

The problem with marks and grades

Alfie Kohn, a well-known and controversial American educationist, has advised teachers not to grade children while they are learning. Black and Wiliam's research shows his advice is not so wide of the mark.

Most people would accept that grades or marks on their own do not improve achievement and research backs this up. Getting four out of ten tells you that you are not achieving but says nothing about how to do better. But research also suggests that marks and comments do not improve achievement either, while comments on their own do. This seems counter-intuitive; why on earth do marks not raise achievement even when they are accompanied by the comments?

Black and Wiliam believe that, when we are given a mark, our ego kicks in and we simply react emotionally to the mark and fail to register the comments. If our mark is lower than we expected, we need to come to terms with our disappointment. If we do better than we expected, we are elated and keen to celebrate or find out if we have done better than our friends. Either way we ignore the comments. We are in 'ego' rather than 'task' mode.

So the lesson in this for teachers is that, if possible, use comment only marking. Alfie Kohn may have gone too far in suggesting that we should never grade children while they are learning. Black and Wiliam's advice is that as far as possible you should reduce the frequency of the marks and the importance given to them. In primary and early secondary sharing marks with children and parents once a year is enough and when working towards national examinations in middle and upper secondary once a term is appropriate.

This is controversial advice that seems impossible to take. Pupils have become marks junkies, craving them all the time, and often supported in the habit by parents. The argument that 'kids need to know where they stand' is true but the real questions are how do we tell them and how often? Children generally know how well they are doing: they certainly don't need to be reminded about it all the time, especially if they lack confidence and are struggling to achieve.

Problems with corrections and comments

Evidence from school inspections throughout the UK suggest that teachers are conscientious but unfocused in their marking. Other criticisms are about where most marking takes place and the lack of opportunity for children to do something about the corrections and comments made:

- marking too many aspects of a piece of work such as content, style, spelling, grammar, and handwriting. This overwhelms children and turns them off,
- making too many general unfocused comments such as 'You need to give a better description here' without offering any idea of what is needed to improve it and how to go about it,
- marking away from the classroom, so children do not get feedback when they need it and by the time they get an opportunity to follow up on corrections and comments, they have lost their currency,
- allowing little or no time during lessons for children to read or follow-up on comments, in order to make small focused improvements based on the comments themselves.

Three strategies to mark less and achieve more

Marking less to achieve more doesn't happen in isolation from the other classroom strategies to improve assessment for learning. Yet the issue of marking effectively can be a good starting point to focus on some of the key principles involved. For example, the real purpose of marking is to give good feedback to children about how well they did against a specific learning intention and some ideas about how they can improve. To make good use of our marking, learners need to know what it tells them and how they should respond to it. Teachers can use three strategies to help develop these skills in learners.

DO MORE MARKING WITH THE WHOLE CLASS

Whole class activities, such as modelling using a specific example of a learner's work can help pupils practise using learning targets or intentions, success criteria and specific ground rules when marking their own work or participating in peer-assessment.

In work that has only one right answer – e.g. in sums and spelling – children can find their own mistakes and make their own corrections. They will need some guidance in where to look for the wrong answers e.g. one out of these five sums is wrong, or 'sp' at the end of a line or a paragraph.

Children can also be supported in marking their own work by providing prompt sheets to help them focus on the important points.

DO LESS MARKING YOURSELF AWAY FROM PUPILS

Classroom situations can be created to allow teachers to give immediate verbal feedback or short written comments while working with groups or individuals.

White space in jotters can be used to write a prompt to help children improve their work. This can be at different levels:

- a reminder ("say more about"),
- a question ("can you describe how"),
- an example (offer a choice of actual words or phrases).

WHEN YOU DO MARK MAKE SURE THAT IT COUNTS

Use comment only marking as much as possible, and only give marks when necessary.

Don't focus on too many things in the one piece of work. Corrections and comments should put responsibility back onto the pupil who should spend more time responding to your marking than you spend doing it. They will need time in class to respond, too.

Challenge more able children by not giving them a grade, but a plus, a minus or an equals depending on how it compares with their last piece of work.

7   TUNING INTO LEARNERS' MINDS

It is the responsibility for diagnosing educational needs that lifts the teacher's work out of the category of routine instruction into that of a highly respected professional.
The Primary Memorandum 1965

It's an essential part of good teaching

TUNING into a learner's mind to clarify what learning has taken place, to identify what learning difficulties are being experienced and to introduce future tasks is one of the biggest challenges for classroom teachers.

Knowing what another person is thinking is difficult. A whole school of psychology did not believe it possible to read other people's minds. It was better, they said, to focus on behaviour and to help people change that.

Thankfully psychology has moved on and we now recognise the importance of tuning into learners' minds and of helping them to understand what's going on there too. It's also easier in a sense, because we understand a great deal more now about how our brains learn than we did when behaviourist approaches were fashionable. Neurology has helped us see how we think things through to come to our current understanding of the world. It has also added weight to the idea that teachers cannot do the learning for their students. Rather, they have a key role in 'mediating' or 'scaffolding' learning.

There are only two ways to do it

Mind-reading apart, there are only two ways to tune into someone else's mind: you can listen to what they say and you can watch what they do. In a well-run classroom, there are plenty of opportunities to do this. As Derek Rowntree points out:

> *The learning situation is awash with process – the on-going reality of students interacting with ideas, with one another, with the teacher and with the physical environment, displaying as they do the workings of their minds and spirits in how they define and respond to the situation they are living through. Some of this may be faintly echoed in whatever products they emerge with. But we can learn much more about students if we observe how they learn and produce.*

A teacher's role is to create opportunities to listen to, discuss with and question individuals, groups and classes. It is also to devise situations for observing individuals and groups at work. Observation when learners are not aware of it is particularly valuable, because it helps to uncover how they think and feel, what makes them 'tick'.

But it's not easy for teachers to get beyond instruction

Research evidence suggests that teachers are not good at diagnosing. A fundamental problem seems to be teachers' preference for immediate instruction rather than for the sustained use of diagnostic activity.
Stevenson and Palmer

Researchers speculate on the reasons why teachers are weak in diagnosing or analysing learners' needs: it may be because they are unaware of its importance, because they believe that it is not necessary since the problems that pupils are having are usually obvious or simply because they lack the skills. For me, it is far more likely that the classroom strategies teachers actually use do not allow them the time or the opportunity for this kind of work.

Panel 6

The teacher's addiction to the right answer

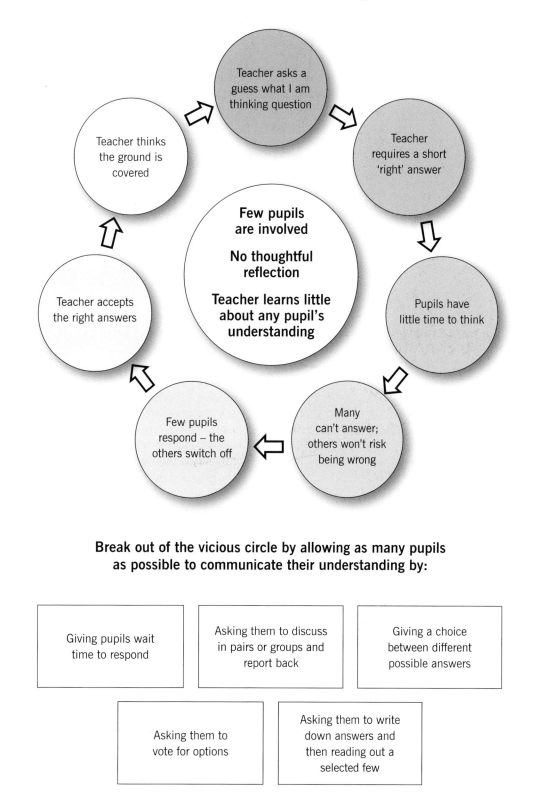

Teacher asks a guess what I am thinking question

Teacher requires a short 'right' answer

Pupils have little time to think

Many can't answer; others won't risk being wrong

Few pupils respond – the others switch off

Teacher accepts the right answers

Teacher thinks the ground is covered

Few pupils are involved

No thoughtful reflection

Teacher learns little about any pupil's understanding

Break out of the vicious circle by allowing as many pupils as possible to communicate their understanding by:

Giving pupils wait time to respond	Asking them to discuss in pairs or groups and report back	Giving a choice between different possible answers
	Asking them to vote for options	Asking them to write down answers and then reading out a selected few

Rowntree's description of process is well understood in the nursery, where analysis and diagnosis is part and parcel of helping young children learn. But as children move up the system and become young adults, the pressure on teachers to instruct reduces opportunities for the richer kinds of communication with which teachers can develop the skills they need to mediate and scaffold learning.

The emphasis on assessing products rather than processes through tests and examinations encourages teachers to look at what children are writing in their exercise books and what they say in response to 'guess what I am thinking' questions. At root, the evidence teachers need to show they are doing a good job is the learner's ability to produce in written or oral form the right answers to a problem set by the teacher. Hence, teachers need a right answer (see panel 6) and the goal for the pupil is to provide an answer that pleases the teacher.

Ironically, to achieve this, learners have to guess what the teacher is thinking, to get into the teacher's mind rather than the other way about!

Practical ways to go beyond instruction

Getting beyond instruction is about using different classroom strategies to encourage quality discussions in pairs, larger groups or the whole class.

This involves creating a climate in the classroom where learners can and do come up with ideas, think out loud, explain their reasoning and explore their understanding, however incomplete, confused or 'way out' they may be.

To get started, teachers need to change their normal classroom behaviour in sometimes simple but always fundamental ways:

- in how they ask questions (Panel 7),
- in how they respond to pupils,
- in the kinds of rituals and routines they use in the classroom,
- in the nature of the tasks and activities they ask learners to undertake.

Teachers often find that quite small changes in how they approach classroom activities can make a significant difference. For instance, they might:

- leave more 'wait time' after asking a question,
- instead of correcting a wrong answer, take the question round the class to tease it out,
- change the hands up rule on occasions to 'no hands up except to ask a question',
- use thumbs to check for understanding after explaining something (thumbs up – understand, thumbs down – don't understand, thumbs across – not sure),
- use 'think, pair and share' regularly during class lessons (think about an answer initially as an individual, then join up with a partner to share ideas, then either pair up again with another pair and repeat the process or report answers back to a larger group).

These may be small ideas, but some are radically different from what children may be used to. For this reason, the teachers on the King's College project, found that it worked best if they started afresh with a new class and explained how they were going to work differently and why.

Panel 7

Ask better questions

To focus attention
Have you seen? What is that?
To force comparisons
How many? How long? How often? How much?
To get clarification
What do you mean by? Can you show me?
Can you explain further? Give me an example?
To stimulate enquiry
What would happen if?
What do we need to know?
To get reasons
How do you know? Why do you think that?

How to improve your questioning

Get better answers

Provide thinking time

A longer wait time (e.g. 3 seconds):
- produces more and better answers,
- allows the learner to think things through,
- shows that responsibility for thinking is with them not you,
- shows that trying takes time and effort and you believe they can do it.

Make questions a habit for learners

Create a questioning climate in class

- Be a role model: ask yourself questions aloud in class – share curiosity and doubts,
- Use books, objects and other items to stimulate questions,
- Encourage learners to bring you objects or issues that interest them,
- Use provocative open-ended questions to stimulate other questions.

8 PROVIDING GOOD QUALITY FEEDBACK

Feedback or knowledge of results is the lifeblood of learning
Derek Rowntree

IT'S not only educationists who recognise the fundamental importance of feedback in learning. In *'Developing Differentiation Practices'* (*The Curriculum Journal*, 1997), Mary Simpson quoted an eleven year old as saying:

> *If teachers would just sit down with you and tell you how you are doing and things. And if you are not good at something, tell you what you could do. I know I'm not good at spelling. She just says "You'll need to work at your spelling", but I don't know how to.*

Constructive feedback on weaknesses and strengths together with advice on how to deal with them will help all children learn. Immediate sincere praise for one child's wild idea during a brainstorming session can give other children the confidence to come up with ideas and think outside the box. Good feedback motivates, while the lack of it turns people off. Many pupils get anxious and bored and act up because they are starved of feedback. With rich feedback, motivation problems disappear. Supportive feedback builds self-esteem and sends messages to children about their effectiveness and worth.

Yet evidence from inspections over the years shows that many classrooms are not particularly rich sources of feedback especially feedback that helps children evaluate their own work and identify what or how to improve. In general, most feedback is too **little**, too **late**, too **vague** and too **impersonal**.

Giving sensitive and effective feedback is a highly developed skill that takes place within a relationship, not a vacuum. It's also one that, as teachers, we pick up on the job from finding out what seems to work for us. Our style of giving feedback tends to reflect our own personality and we don't have many opportunities to examine and reflect on it.

Much of the advice given to teachers over the years has been simplistic or contradictory. They have been asked to be more positive and to 'praise more'. Yet at the same time they have been told that feedback needs to be realistic and sincere.

Perhaps the concept of praise itself is less of a problem than the kind of praise we use in schools. Teachers often use praise after a task has been completed and it tends to be judgemental. Judgements often get in the way of relationships. Indeed there is some research to show that what irritates teenagers about their parents more than anything else is being judged. Yet a lot of the time we do not need to judge or praise; other strategies can be more effective. For example, we can just take an interest in what a child is doing or we can simply describe in a clear and detailed way what we see.

Regular, excessive praise often does more harm than good, leading to delusion or even frustration and resentment. To be effective, praise must confirm a child's own sense of reality. Even young children are remarkably good at working out what 'doing well' means - much more so than many adults appreciate. Children who are told from an early age that everything they make or do is wonderful and that they are really clever, can become confused and unable to develop their own critical judgement. They can even come to resent indiscriminate praise. Instead, parents and teachers need to help children develop their own standards of performance.

Alan McLean *(The Motivated School)* uses the term 'plastic praise' to help teachers realise that they should use praise less and encouragement more. Encouragement doesn't judge, it needn't be earned, and it can be given at any time for any reason.

To improve classroom feedback, we need much more than exhortations and general advice. We need to be aware of how we come across to others. Words are only a small part of the feedback we give constantly to other people: our facial expressions, the warmth in our eyes, the gestures we use and our general body language speak more loudly than words.

It can also help to be more aware of two kinds of feedback (Panel 8): 'descriptive' or 'task-centred' feedback and 'supportive' or 'person-centred' feedback. One of the critical balancing acts in teaching is getting the right balance between the two for the occasion and for the individual child or class you are working with.

In real life, the two types are hardly ever separate from each other. You could be giving descriptive feedback verbally while your body language is supportive, for instance. But they are different in nature and purpose.

For example, a wide body of research on psychological type suggests that although we all want and need both kinds of feedback, we tend to have a natural preference for one or the other. Most importantly, we tend to give others more of the kind of feedback that we like to get ourselves, even though that person might actually need the other kind.

Panel 8

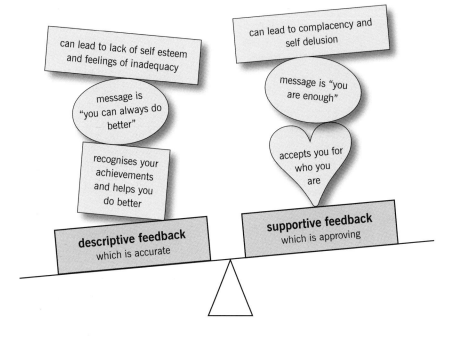

Descriptive feedback is valued most by people with a strong drive for competence. They want recognition for their achievements, but feel patronised if they are praised for something they don't feel is good. If self-confident, they will see criticism as a means to improvement. When giving feedback, they may be over critical and not take people's feelings into account. When faced with a problem they tend to be tough-minded, to focus on the task in hand and to think logically and objectively. Providing effective descriptive feedback then involves:

* listening first and listening more,
* taking students' questions seriously,
* giving fewer direct and instant responses to students' queries,
* asking questions that invite students to examine their thinking,
* making comments that stimulate thinking,
* slowing down the pace of conversations to leave time for thinking.

Supportive feedback is valued most by people who need to be accepted for who they are rather than for what they can do. They need positive feedback, encouragement and appreciation, particularly if they lack self-confidence. When giving feedback they may avoid being critical because of a concern for how the person will feel. When faced with a problem or an issue they tend to be sympathetic and accepting and to focus on values and how people will be affected by any solution. Effective supportive feedback:

* focuses on effort not ability,
* gives fewer judgements and more opinions,
* gives less Lpraise and more encouragement,
* includes your expectations but not pushed or hammered home with too many shoulds or oughts or musts,
* encourages young people to use empowering language,
* avoids pushing positive thinking too much.

9   TAKING SELF AND PEER ASSESSMENT SERIOUSLY

Assessment by pupils, far from being a luxury is an essential part of formative assessment.
Paul Black and Dylan Wiliam *Inside the Black Box*

Why develop self and peer assessment?

THERE are three reasons why we should teach children to assess their own and each other's work regularly.

The first is pragmatic. To learn effectively we all need good, continuous feedback, tailored to our individual needs. If all the feedback in a classroom of thirty pupils has to come through the teacher there will be a bottleneck - a queue at the teacher's desk - and good feedback for all pupils all of the time becomes impossible. For this reason alone, an effective assessment system must include elements of self or peer assessment.

The second is for learners. Monitoring your own progress against goals is a valuable skill in its own right. It helps learners develop an awareness of how they learn and promotes better learning.

The last is for teachers. If learners can reflect accurately and honestly on their own work, the evidence generated can provide teachers with information to back up their own judgements and give them valuable insights into their learners' thinking, leading to more effective teaching.

What are the drawbacks?

There can be very few. Research shows that children of five and younger can self-assess with great skill if they are taught how to do so. They are also keen to do so if they see it as part of learning, helping them to learn more effectively. In this atmosphere, pupils are generally honest in assessing both themselves and others. In fact, they are often too hard on themselves.

But as pupils move up the system, their attitude towards assessment tends to change. It becomes associated with getting grades and competing with one another. Teachers and pupils can regard self and peer assessment as a 'skivers charter' and do not take it seriously. Without a well-established habit of self and peer assessment and the associated skills to work with, introducing effective self and peer assessment can be very difficult.

How to develop peer and self assessment

Learners need three things to assess themselves and their peers effectively. If one is missing, they will not succeed. If all are present then, eventually, even children who are unwilling to take assessment seriously will discover its benefits. The three things are:

- information about what they need to learn and how they will know they have been successful,
- a greater understanding of what constitutes quality work,
- the skills and techniques required to assess what they have achieved.

Providing information

To help children engage in their own assessment, teachers need to go beyond simply telling students what to do and how to do it (**the task or activity**). Research shows teachers are good at this but not so good at making clear what is to be learned (**the learning intention or outcome**) and how to recognise success (**the success criteria**).

Developing an understanding of quality

Teachers need to find ways to talk about quality all the time. Pupils need to know what quality work looks like at different levels. They need to know why their work is at level C and, more importantly, they need to know how to get to the next level.

Some ways to do this might be to:

- examine the marking process for a class by using a piece of work from another class or a previous year group. The example could be projected on an overhead,
- discuss the differences between two pieces of work with the same title but at different levels.

Practising skills and techniques

One way to practise self and peer assessment skills in a class is to hold regular debriefing sessions at the end of lessons. A range of self-evaluation questions can be displayed on the board or on a poster and they can be linked to learning intentions and success criteria. A session can deal with the answers the children might have been pleased with or look for other suggestions.

In *Unlocking Formative Assessment*, Shirley Clarke suggests that debriefing should be conducted orally and avoid asking children to write their responses as their thinking will then be reduced to what they can write.

Panel 9

Taking self and peer assessment seriously

If self and peer assessment is to be fully utilised, particularly in secondary schools, it needs to be taken seriously by individual teachers and the school as a whole. So:

Build it in. Self-assessment can be a natural and habitual component of day-to-day activities, not a separate one-off exercise or event.

Give it time and space. Children need time to self-assess and to act on what they discover. In a crowded curriculum, this may mean taking a stand and deciding to cover less ground especially in literacy and numeracy.

Keep it varied. Don't let self-assessment activities become tedious, onerous or just routine. Keep them continually under review and ask for feedback on them from pupils on a regular basis.

Show that it works. Create a climate where pupils see the point of self-assessment and value it, rather than seeing it as a 'skivers charter' Help them to understand and experience the benefits of honest self-assessment in helping them to learn.

Value it. Give self-assessment high status by trusting the results and taking them seriously yourself (e.g. when setting goals with pupils and making individualised instructional decisions) and when reporting to parents.

Teach self-assessment techniques. Self-assessment, like everything else, needs to be developed. Start small and keep things simple. Expose pupils to a range of techniques and opportunities to practise, refine and personalise them.

Engage pupils regularly in dialogue about their learning. Pupils will only be able to use self-assessment techniques effectively if they are helped to enlarge their repertoire of ways of thinking about their learning and the vocabulary needed to talk about it. Opportunities to help pupils to express their understandings should be built into any piece of teaching. All pupils should have a chance to think and express their ideas.

Make it lead somewhere. Self-assessment and goal setting are closely linked. If pupils do not know why they are learning and the targets they are expected to achieve, they will not be able to self-assess nor will they be motivated to do so.

Focus on strengths. Self-assessment should help build pupils' self-confidence. Make it an affirmative exercise. Areas of support and attention obviously have to be identified but are best dealt with in the context of an honest acknowledgement of strengths and accomplishments.

IO

RECONCILING THE USES OF ASSESSMENT

Improvement and accountability can be interwoven.
Michael Fullan

WE urgently need to take steps at all stages in the education system, but particularly in secondary education to reconcile the conflicting demands for improvement and accountability. For this to happen, a polarised and simplistic 'either-or' debate about assessment as improvement or accountability, feedback or results, profiling or testing has to be replaced by a real dialogue about both formative and summative assessment and how the two can work together. This dialogue needs to flow though every part of the education system.

Reconciliation at classroom level: checking up and summing up

Assessing pupils for external purposes is clearly different from assessing their on-going work to monitor and improve progress. Summative assessment tends to cast the teacher in the role of judge, formative assessment in the role of facilitator.

Some have argued that the two roles are so different they should be kept apart but this is simply not practical for teachers or pupils, and would actually have harmful effects on both teachers and education generally. The challenge is to develop a more positive relationship between the two in the classroom and to ensure that the demands of summative assessment do not outweigh the benefits offered by formative assessment:

> *Continuous assessment cannot function formatively when it is cumulative, that is, when each attempt or piece of work submitted is scored and the scores are added together at the end of the course. This practice tends to produce in students the mindset that if a piece of work does not contribute towards the total, it is not worth doing.*
> **Saddler** (1989) quoted in **Caroline Gipps** *'Beyond Testing'*

One way to achieve a balance is to make a distinction between two different kinds of summative assessment, namely 'checking up' and 'summing up' (Harlen et al 1992 quoted in Caroline Gipps *'Beyond Testing'*). 'Checking up' is about testing, which can be considered separately from information used for summative purposes. 'Summing up' is about the process of bringing together information collected over a period of time and already used for formative purposes to provide a picture of current achievement. This distinction allows the use of formative assessment for summative purposes without impairing its feedback role.

By making a distinction like this, schools can begin to satisfy the need for interim measurement against targets as they go along. However, these measurements can be done at school and class level, not at that of an individual child.

Reconciliation at national level: improvement and accountability

Without reconciling the tensions between improvement and accountability at national level, balancing the two in school and classrooms will always be a difficult job. The debate nationally should not simply focus on how to raise standards but must fundamentally be about the standards we want. Unless we are clear about what we want from our schools and our education system, we can't know the standards we seek. To work together, each side of the argument needs to see where the other is coming from. As Stephen Covey says, each must 'seek first to understand' the other's position.

Those who would emphasise improvement must recognise that:

1   all results either bad or good are ultimately good because they provide us with feedback to guide us about what to do next and how to do it better: processes exist for results and results should inform processes.

2   ultimately learning is judged by results and the issue of assessment is about knowing how and when to measure these results.

3   tests and examinations have a part to play in any education system, but we need to make them more valid and reliable especially in the area of soft skills such as teamworking and collaboration. We need to understand that some skills cannot be assessed effectively through formal tests and examinations.

4   accountability must run right through the system. Children and their parents have a right to know how things are going in school. Headteachers need to know how well teachers are working and our elected representatives have a duty to know how well schools are performing.

Those who would emphasise accountability must recognise that:

1   without goals for our education system we do not know what the important results are. In education, the important goals tend to be long term and difficult to measure by quantitative measures alone.

2   there is no such thing as a true score. Assessment is not scientific and we should stop presenting it as such. For instance, it is ludicrous to claim that a result on a one-off test on a twelve year old can predict what his or her grade will be in an examination four years later.

3   to effect improvement, users must engage with the standards set. This won't happen if they believe them to be at odds with what they as learners and teachers aspire to and believe to be possible.

4   simply setting standards will not work. People need encouragement and support in working towards goals even when they know they are worthwhile.

A lot can and is being done at the grass roots in schools and classrooms. However, we need to engage in a public debate. People working in the education system should be willing to take the lead of the Assessment Reform Group and establish such a dialogue. Only by showing that we can balance accountability and improvement in classrooms will we win back the trust lost in the early seventies.

Panel 10

Reducing the threat from a focus on results at school level

Wrongly used, setting goals and gathering information about how far these goals have been achieved "can have a chilling effect" which can drive out team working and uninhibited knowledge sharing.

But teachers are only genuine professionals if they are accountable to their clients and to society at large. A school needs to produce the learning results required by the community. Parents and community leaders must have some kind of product that will persuade them that schools are performing the way they want them to perform. Until educators develop such products, test scores will continue to dominate the thinking of many outside school.

We need to reduce the threat from setting goals and using data without eliminating accountability by the following strategies:

1   do not introduce high stakes prematurely.

2   collect and analyse data collaboratively and anonymously by team, department, grade level or school. Ensure that those closest to the point of implementation - the practitioners - analyse the data. In other words let the team exercise its own accountability.

3   do not use data primarily to identify or eliminate poor teachers.

4   avoid introducing any idea of performance related pay or using data for evaluation, use the data for improvement purposes only.

5   if data are to be used for evaluation institute a true appeal system which allows schools or teams to "reject, if necessary, targets handed down to them" (Tom Peters).

6   allow teachers by school or team as much autonomy as possible in selecting the kind of data they think will be most helpful.

7   inundate teachers with success stories that include data. The stories should show how we achieve success when we select the right goals - manageable ones - and employ the best strategies for reaching them.

Taken from **Schmoker**: *'Results'*

II   IS THE TIDE TURNING?

Across the world there is a growing challenge to conventional testing.
Paul Black and Dylan Wiliam *Inside the Black Box*

I FERVENTLY hope that Black and Wiliam are right and that the challenge to testing means that the assessment tide is on the turn. *Inside the Black Box* and other work from Kings College have begun to spawn an encouraging grass roots movement among teachers and other educationists. The Assessment Reform Group has produced *Ten Research-based Principles to Guide Classroom Practice in Assessment for Learning* in 2002 and *Beyond the Black Box*, a six-point plan for national action.

These are promising signs but it is easy to be sceptical about their eventual impact. Our current assessment system may be a focus of complaint from teachers but many still use the assessment system as a reason, perhaps even an excuse for focusing on instruction rather than learning and for not helping children to take responsibility for their own learning.

Perhaps it is a good excuse. It's not easy to help children used to being spoon fed to take responsibility for their own learning and assess themselves and their peers. It takes skill and persistence and a belief in young people and yourself as a teacher. It's not easy in areas of systemic under-achievement and no less difficult in more affluent areas where pressure for good examination results is high. What if you try it and the results suffer? Accusations of bad teaching or worse? Best to take the safe and easy option.

It's a vicious circle and we will not help all young people to reach their full potential until we break out of it. But scanning the shore for a turn in the assessment tide is not to argue that standards or results don't matter, that examinations and testing have no place in a national assessment system. Nor is it to argue for a return to times when schools and teachers were not accountable, or to disregard the real concerns for basic standards felt in the aftermath of earlier changes in teaching methods.

But Black and Wiliam are right in their central thesis. If we let the present assessment tide run, we will soon reach a ceiling in standards of literacy and numeracy well below what many young people are capable of. Other critical skills like creativity and team working which we hold dear will continue to be underdeveloped in school.

I'll leave the last word to David Hargreaves speaking to a conference of educational researchers. Addressing the common complaint that we assess too much, he said:

> *It is not said enough that we assess too little, that is, assess too narrow a range of human abilities and skills by far too limited methods, mainly pencil and paper tests. More creative blue skies work by researchers on what can be assessed and how it might be better assessed would be very welcome.*

Hargreaves was calling for more people to take up what Black and Wiliam had begun. In closing this paper, it's worth repeating his call. *Inside the Black Box* is founded on the experience of real teachers and learners in real classrooms; it now needs many more of them to carry its message forward.

REFERENCES AND FURTHER READING

References

Guy Claxton *'Wise Up'*, Bloomsbury, 2000

Michael Fullan and Andy Hargreaves *'What's Worth Fighting for in Your School?'*, OU Press, Buckingham, 1992

David Hargreaves *'The Future of Educational Research'*, paper presented at BERA conference, 2001

Assessment in Education Volume 5 Number 1 March 1998 Special Issue on *Assessment and Classroom Learning*, Carfax Publishing Ltd., PO Box 25, Abingdon, Oxfordshire.

Alfie Kohn *'Punished by Rewards'*, Houghton, Mifflin & Co, Ney Your, 1993

Alan McLean *'The Motivated School'*, Sage publications, 2003

Andrew Pollard and Sarah Tann *Reflective Teaching in the Primary School*, Cassell, London, 1987

Derek Rowntree *'Assessing Students: How Shall We Know Them?'*, Kogan Page, London, 1987

Scottish Education Department *'The Primary Memorandum'*, 1965

Scottish Office Education Department *'Assessment 5-14'*, 1991

Frank Smith *'The Book of Learning and Forgetting'*, Teachers College Press, New York, 1998

Stevenson and Palmer *'Learning Principles: Processes and Priorities'*, Cassell, London, 1994

Mary Simpson *'Developing Differentiation Practices'*, The Curriculum Journal 1997

Harry Torrance and John Pryor *'Investigating Formative Assessment'*, Open University Press, Buckingham, 1998

Lev Vygotsky *'Mind in Society'*, Harvard University Press, 1978

Colin Weatherley et al *Transforming Teaching and Learning: Developing Critical Skills for Living and Working in the 21st Century'*, Network Press, 2003

Dylan Wiliam *'Integrating Formative and Summative Assessment'*, paper presented at International Congress on Mathematics Education in Tokyo, August, 2000

Dylan Wiliam *'Teachers Developing Assessment for Learning: Impact on student achievement'*, paper presented at BERA conference, 2001

Further reading

'Assessment for Learning: Beyond the black box', **Assessment Reform Group**, Cambridge, 1999

Paul Black *'Testing: Friend or Foe'*, Falmer Press, London, 1998.

Paul Black, Christine Harrison, Clare Lee, Bethan Marshall and Dylan Wiliam *'Working Inside the Black Box'*, Kings College, London, 2002

Paul Black and Dylan Wiliam *'Inside the Black Box: Raising standards through classroom assessment'*, Kings College, London, 1998

Shirley Clarke *'Targeting Assessment in the Primary Classroom'*, Hodder and Stoughton, Abingdon, 1998

Shirley Clarke *'Unlocking Formative Assessment'* Hodder and Stoughton, Abingdon, 2001

Mary Jane Drummond *'Assessing Children's Learning'*, David Fulton, 1994

Caroline Gipps *'Beyond Testing: Towards a Theory of Educational Assessment'*, Falmer Press, 1994

Mike Schmoker *'Results: The Key to Continuous Improvement'*, ASCD, Alexandria, Virginia, 1996

'Testing, Motivation and Learning', **Assessment Reform Group**, Cambridge, 2002